Table of Contents

Greetings fellow Cat Partiers! ... 1
Katie Haegele

Cat Party

Coco the Cat ... 2
Keiko Ishibashi

Catty ... 3
Alison Chapman

Kittens and Cocktails ... 6
Raymond E. Mingst

names and nicknames for a cat ... 11
Andrew Keller

The Crime Cats ... 13
Ivan Dellinger

Cartoons' Coolest Cats ... 17
Ed Kemp

Take a Catwalk with Me ... 19
Katie Haegele

Turning into a Cat ... 21
Jo-Jo Sherrow

Meet the Contributors ... 22

Greetings fellow Cat Partiers!

I'm so glad you're here. I have a new batch of work that I'm excited to share with you, artwork and stories and comics made by friends and friendly others whose work I really admire. One of the reasons I connect to their work, of course, is that they are all cat lovers. They understand how special these animals are, and how important our friendships with them can be.

It's been over a year now since my dear cat Coco died, and my partner Joe and I have been living in our stupid house without a cat all this time. Things really aren't the same without her here. I miss the enormous attitude she liked to give me in response to any tiny transgression, like the way she'd stare me down if I was sitting in her preferred spot on the couch, and how she'd get up and leave the room in a huff when Joe and I annoyed her by laughing too loudly. Her peevishness just made me want to please her more. I miss being able to hug her during times of emotional stress, the way just resting my hand on her thick, plush fur seemed to make my blood pressure go down. I probably spent, I don't know, 70% of my time at home just gazing at her—she was so pretty, and endlessly interesting. What a gift to get to share my home with someone of another species! I miss how friendly and fearless she was, especially for an old gal. Whenever we had a party she'd come trundling down the stairs to see everyone, even after the voices and music had gotten loud and boisterous. I also get a warm feeling when I remember her in our tiny backyard, curled up under the blueberry bush, practically beaming pure joy and contentment. Whether she was feeling solitary or sociable, pleased or grouchy, she really was a cat for all seasons.

These days Joe and I have been home less and traveling more. We've been trying to find our place in the world, since our understanding of that seems to have shifted a bit ever sense the world was picked up and shaken like a snow globe a few years ago. It's a work in progress—whose life isn't?—but the point is, we don't want to open up our home to another cat until we feel more settled and can be as attentive and devoted to that creature as he or she deserves. For now I will have to get my cat needs met by visiting my buddies in the neighborhood (see my piece "Take a Cat Walk with Me" for more on that) and from the contributions to these Cat Party anthologies, which are always so sweet, sad, funny, and real. I extend my thanks to the artists who shared them, and to you for picking up the zine. I consider us to be a kind of community, a scattershot worldwide community of humans who really dig cats, and it feels good to be among friends.

—Katie Haegele, Philadelphia
January 2023

Keiko Ishibashi

Catty

Alison Chapman

The year after my father died, my sister rescued a kitten from drowning in a flooded window well. She brought it to my parents' house, where it hid under the furniture for weeks. My mom didn't know if we were keeping it or if my sister would find it a new home. We figured it would stay, at least for while, because who wants a kitten that's afraid of the world? So, we left food and water nearby and waited for it to come out.

I had moved back to my parents' house to stay for a while, unsure of how long. Life without my dad seemed vast, in that terrifying, gasping way—like treading water in the middle of the ocean. In the wake of my dad's passing, my childhood home was one of those after-shock blankets you'd get in the back of an ambulance, something to cling to that's life affirming. I couldn't find peace anywhere else.

As I milled through my days, the cat ventured out from hiding, lurking around my bedroom. She would sit on the windowsill, enjoying the sunshine from her safe space, occasionally looking in my direction, blinking slowly.

I called her Catty, a joke based on her spiteful disposition. She tolerated a few tender moments here and there, allowing a minute or two of chin scratches until she decided that it was enough, and she would abruptly sulk away.

I couldn't blame her for the way she was—her earliest memories are of almost dying. I'm not sure traumatized cats can force optimism upon themselves, and I'm not sure they should, either. Optimism doesn't help small animals stay alive.

Eventually I enrolled in art school in Philadelphia. I hated leaving my mom's house, and leaving Catty behind. But in forcing optimism upon myself, I had decided that this was the right step towards something like moving forward. Catty had gotten braver too, taking short ventures into the yard. I watched her courage grow as she tentatively explored the tall grasses behind the house.

Some time after I moved, my mom told me that Catty had gone out all the way into the woods and hadn't come back. I waited for news of her eventual return, but the news never came.

Had Catty gone looking for me? Was I the only thing that kept her at the house? Or had she even noticed I was gone?

Who knows how long she survived out there, in full view of hawks and coyotes. It's possible that her hiding skills and mistrust of every living thing kept her alive longer than the average escaped house pet. Maybe she lived fifteen more years, a silent hunter, a ghost of the forest. A survivor.

I still keep my eye out for her when I visit home. It's been almost 20 years, though—so now when I walk through those woods, I imagine her spirit, an apparition, darting between thickets along the forest's edge. For every dead field mouse carcass I come across, I wonder if it's her offering from the afterlife.

I tell her, wherever she is, that I'm sorry I left. I am sorry if her adventures led to her being carried off, full of fear, to the end of her life.

But I'm not sorry if when she left, she thrived, unburdened and finally unafraid.

Kittens and Cocktails

Raymond E. Mingst

My handshake is neither limp, nor crushing. It is firm. My posture is good. One doesn't eat food while walking down the street, nor would you comb your hair while out in public. These are some of the lessons my parents taught me. The ones I remember best were those taught earliest, perhaps when I was about 5 years old. I appreciated knowing how to be in society; the expectations, what it was to be kind and confident, thoughtful, polite. Certainly, the guidance was meant to help me through life, offer tools to navigate every sort of interaction and situation. Also, to express who I was and what I represented — my identity and place in the world.

Another lesson: on any occasion, you should always be prepared and able to contribute in one way or another. I was not precocious, but I was also taught how to properly mix a cocktail. Tending to guests with a Tom Collins is a useful skill for a child. The hosts, my parents, wouldn't have to interrupt the flow of drinks or conversation. (Fill the glass with ice, use the first cube as a guide for how much alcohol to pour, mixer, stir, garnish.) As a child, I don't recall objecting to any of these teachings. They seemed reasonable, civilized; how a good person would behave and treat others. I accepted them all, uncritically. In retrospect I realize these life lessons were colored by my parents mid-twentieth century notions of what is proper, what is good, clean, and orderly.

Understanding what was 'good' meant, naturally, that some things were 'bad.' Some things were to be avoided, were counter to our way of being (which was the correct way). I admit these particular prejudices — what was bad — I accepted as full truth. And here I'm going to confront one of those prejudices. I recall my mother stating more than once, and absolutely: "The homes of people with cats smell." Also, to me: "you would never want a cat." I'd never expressed to my parents a desire to have a cat, but somehow among the many ways we defined and presented ourselves, the distinction of being 'dog people' rather than 'cat people' was one to note. Should the question ever arise, I could blithely identify as a dog person since there was nothing at stake for me.

Along the way and as an adult, I'd visited the homes of friends who had a cat, or multiple cats, even dogs and cats. The cats as a whole seemed as indifferent to me as I was to them. I didn't dislike them; they were simply benign presences. They might walk across your lap if they felt like it, but they didn't require any attention. Dogs liked to be petted. Cats, it seemed to me, did not.

When I met my partner, A., he didn't have any pets. (I had a tiny frog and a couple finches. Which, as I write this, suddenly seems telling. Of what I don't know.) With A., the dog person / cat person conversation didn't happen until we'd decided to move in together. We'd been together while keeping our own spaces in the East Village of Manhattan for quite a few years. But this was real moving in together, getting a place of our own to share.

As it turned out, A. is a cat person. He had always had a cat. Growing up, his family had numerous cats that came and went following their whim or hunger. Almost immediately upon moving into our new, very old, home, A. expressed his desire to adopt one. This was a wrinkle I hadn't expected. I knew I didn't want a smelly home. So, I managed to avoid the issue deftly for several years, calling upon the dangerous and dust-producing renovations we were taking on. The conditions would be unhealthy for a pet, and it was a solid argument. However, we eventually got things in relatively good order and a cat seemed perfectly feasible. Also, the issue of odor wasn't confirmed by anyone I knew with cats, so beyond a very faint, lingering filial duty to honor a canine over feline affinity — which I'd eventually confront with my parents — I didn't have particular objections. So sure, let's get a cat.

We started at Liberty Humane Society in Jersey City where we'd moved. A. had an idea of the type of cat he wanted (he insists some cats can have a green cast to their coats, and that's what we were looking for), while my only request was that we adopt a kitten. I figured any potential neurotic behavior should be a result of living with us, not someone else. Right off, I liked a friendly black and white cat we met there, but since this was to be A.'s cat I wanted to be sure we found exactly the cat he was looking for, a green cat, whatever that meant. We didn't have luck in Jersey City, so we crossed back over the river and learned kitten season starts more or less in the spring. We'd made looking for a cat a regular weekend activity. I believe we'd started in the winter, not ideal. We set about visiting shelters, all virtually empty, filling out lengthy forms along the way. We started downtown and proceeded up. Finally, one weekend we'd reached Animal Care and Control at 110th Street to be told yet again there were no kittens. While we were there, we decided to nose around. There was a family scouting for a kitten too and as a group we went into rooms with stacked cages that felt a bit off limits, but no one was around to object.

Sure enough, in an otherwise empty room of cages, one was filled with a pile of sleeping kittens. The moment A. and I looked into the cage the kitten laying on top lifted his head, looked at us, meowed, and we instantly agreed he was the guy for us. The family poking around beside us adopted too. These brothers all quickly found homes. I can't truly and honestly say our tabby kitten had a greenish cast to his coat but in certain light we thought maybe. After very lengthy debate we named the kitten Coven (long o) Ko-vhen. (It's a reference to the documentary "American Movie".)

Since bringing Coven home I can't imagine a home without a cat. Coven activated our home, made it alive. Coven was very beautiful even though he's supposedly a common sort. People found him remarkable, I can't say why exactly, but it was true. He would inspire comments on his appeal while simply laying down doing nothing.

The first night we brought Coven home I worried about him not having the comfort of another heartbeat to sleep with. So, I slept on the bathroom floor with him nestled next to me. A. was an old hand with cats and had no worries, but I was new to this. Coven was very tiny and had such big ears. His markings were elegant and symmetrical. I sang songs to Coven constantly, all of which he was the subject. I talked to him; he'd talk too. It delighted me when I'd be upstairs, call his name and he'd poke his head through the banisters to look to me, then pad up to keep me company. I called Coven the best little kitty in the world, and for me he was. Often when I'd work, he'd be on the corner of my drafting table with his head under the warmth of the lamp. I felt both of us content.

The human, animal bond and more specifically why living with a cat is satisfying has certainly been studied; the benefits to our well-being measured and cataloged. I'm confident these studies exist although I haven't read any. I don't have thoughtful insight into the scientific aspect of keeping pets. For me, what I experienced was, I suppose, a kind of first love. Coven belonged to A., but we had our own special bond.

Coven was plagued with some health issues that worried us initially, but we managed. While the general consensus remains that online medical advice is less reliable than a doctor visit, we found it otherwise. Coven had some urinary issues that the vet suggested required exploratory surgery, 'to be sure, and rule some things out'. This seemed creepily opportunistic and sounded like an upsell in treatment designed to take advantage of our attachment. Our online research consistently tied Coven's symptoms to being a neutered male. A special diet was recommended, and it turned out to be an effective treatment. We never returned to that vet.

There were other persistent things, like ear mites, but we treated them. He got worms once too, which was a super disgusting discovery. We think he may have gotten them from eating a mouse. One morning, Coven was in my studio sitting very erect. I said, 'good morning' and he didn't respond, just sat there not moving a muscle. It was strange. I said, 'hey Coven, what's up?' and he didn't move from a spot in the middle of the floor. I got close to him and noticed at his feet a little dead mouse, most of one anyway. Of course, I can't be sure, but I think he was really proud of catching the mouse and was waiting to show me. You may find it ghoulish, but I was indeed very proud and gave him many congratulations.

I've been writing in the past tense, so I'm sure you understand Coven is gone now. My very dear and daily companion lived what I've been told was a good, long life. Thinking of him now, I'm already finding it difficult to type and see the computer screen. Coven was the best little kitty in the world. I loved him very much. And I miss him. I thank you for indulging me in sharing a bit about him. I still have the xerox page from when he was first brought to Animal Care & Control of New York City. The printout has a little picture of tiny Coven in the upper left-hand corner. They gave it to us, along with other documents, when we collected him for the journey from 110th Street in Manhattan to 5th Street in Jersey City. The page details Name: UNKNOWN, Color: BR TIGER & BR TIGER, Breed: DOMESTIC SH, Sex: MALE, Markings: 4 KITTENS IN A BOX, Found at: FD IN BOX 1553 STARLING AV. I sometimes think about visiting Starling Ave. I don't know where that is, but maybe someday.

When Coven came into our lives, I knew I'd eventually want to warn my parents of his residency. From them, I was anticipating resigned disappointment. They would manage to communicate their disapproval with veiled politeness. Perhaps they'd start to pause before sitting down anywhere, stealthily examining cushions for the abundance of cat hair that was sure to cover every surface of my home. Scented candles would suddenly become the gift of choice to bring with each visit. I've brought them what I knew would be disappointing news before (I dented the car! I'm a fine arts major! I bought a fixer upper!), so I proceeded with the announcement, prepared to endure the displeasure of these avowed dog people. When I shared that a little kitten was now part of my family their eyes brightened. They were absolutely delighted. I thought, really? But we're dog people. You told me as much. They just smiled and immediately shared the names of each of their own kittens they'd had as children. Wait. What!? You had cats? And the names! Snowball for my mom, and Mittens for my dad (it may have been the other way around,) but really?! My incredulity at the fact that my parents lied to me about cats for all these years was met with what I should have learned from past, similar experiences. There wouldn't be an explanation, or an apology, or denial, or anything other than the two them sharing a sort of conspiratorial laugh and a very particular facial expression which in this case communicated: how in the world would anyone not want an adorable little kitty. Then: why are you always so tense? You're making something of nothing. And finally: Coven, what an unusual name, so fun. Raymond, you should relax more, why don't you go ahead and make us all cocktails.

One last note: the cat currently in residence at our house is named Juan Gris, named for his grey coat and after the Spanish Cubist painter. He has button eyes and is very adorable. He jumps on our heads to wake us every morning and likes attention. Also, if a person who keeps a cat has a home that smells, it is the person's fault, not the cat's.

names and nicknames for a cat, and

Andrew Keller

allentina: formal name, taken from her very vocal nature, or her howl, aka the work by allen ginsberg, and tina turner.

babygirl: the name on the tag of her collar. also her first nickname.

baby: what we call her now.

baby the cat: nice name for a comic book

lil baby: i got really into my turn by lil baby in lockdown. especially songs like "can't explain," and "emotionally scarred."

sweet sweet sweet baby girl - (sung to the tune of the three's company theme song)

bunny: most cats head-butt for affection and pets; the goodest cat (another nickname) hops like a bunny.

bun

bunny buddy

hopper

sweet bun

my sweet bun

bunita: a portmanteau of "bunny" and "bonita," the spanish word for cute planations when necessary.

cloud: she's all white

cloud girl: inspired by "glad girls" by guided by voices. i sing, "hey, cloud girl. only wanna feed you snacks."

cloud belly: from her soft white belly. almost was the name of a food catering business her other human, dana, wants to start.

loaf: baby loves to loaf near the front door.

loafie: like the name sophie

loafer: like the shoe

snuzie: like the name suzie, because she likes to snooze

no-no (for when she does bad stuff)

lc — long cat

elsie

dumpling — a short-lived nickname. rip dumpling the name, not the cat

The
CRIME
I DIDN'T SAVE YOU ANY QUICHE.
VENGEANCE FOR FREYA THE WALRUS.
CATS
ID 2022

By

IVAN DELLINGER

SOME SCULPT, SOME PAINT; MY ART IS BARFING ON THE CLEAN LAUNDRY.
ID 2022
SAVE THE BEES, CLEAN THE SEAS, PLANT MORE TREES, KILL NAZIS.

DON'T TALK TO ME UNTIL I'VE HAD MY SOCIETAL + INDUSTRIAL COLLAPSE.
ID2022

WEED LEGALIZATION WITHOUT DISINCARCERATION + REPARATIONS ONLY SERVES WHITE SUPREMACY + CAPITALISM.
ID2022

Cartoons' Coolest Cats

Ed Kemp

There have been many cartoon cats throughout the years. Some have been in starring roles, like Felix, possibly our first cartoon cat, or Fritz, the bad kitty of cartoons; while others, like Azrael or Figaro, were just supporting characters. All cats are cool, that's without question, but only the coolest of the cool cats made my cut.

5) Tom

Tom's a lovable loser, similar to the Chicago Cubs before they won the World Series back in 2016. I like Tom, but let's face it, he's a dud. He's constantly getting out-smarted, or even worse, out-muscled, by a much smaller creature further down the food chain. In the end though, I guess it's a good thing because if this cartoon played out like real life, it could have been a short and gruesome cartoon series.

4) Chester Cheetah

"It's not easy being cheesy" is almost enough on its own to land Chester on this list, but looking back on old commercials, that wasn't the only sick bar our cartoon Cheetah spit back in the day. Many commercials from my youth had him reciting rhyme after cheesy rhyme, sounding like some sort of beatnik poet, all while being voiced by a Tone Loc impersonator. And if his poetry skills weren't enough, animators had him wear sneakers and sunglasses to emphasize just how cool he really was. Also, Cheetos are way better than Frosted Flakes, which gives Chester the edge over that bandana-wearing, sugary cereal-selling tiger.

3) Snowball II

While not the most major character in the series, often losing screen time to that scene stealing show-off Santa's Little Helper, she is The Simpson's family cat and the show is the greatest cartoon ever, so ipso facto, she's here on the list. But let's not forget about the fact that she does totally belong here. She did, after all, save Homer from that burning treehouse while "man's best friend" turned his cowardly back. Also, there's the time in another episode that she gains a bunch of weight by moonlighting with another family and getting double fed, something that my first cat really did. MacGregor was an indoor/outdoor cat that would sometimes disappear for a week or two at a time, often coming home smelling of smoke, but we could never really figure out why. We theorized that she had a side family that had a camp fire or chain smoked Marlboro Reds or something. Well, after she died, we saw flyers from someone looking for a missing cat fitting my cat's description. My mom called and talked to the "other" family and it turned out that our theory was spot on, our calico cat led a double life with another family for years leading up to her passing.

2) Sylvester

Sly gets a bad rap for hunting the cute, sweet and catch-phrase spewing Tweety Bird, but it is not his fault. HE'S A CAT! He's predisposed to want to hunt birds, it's in his DNA. No, I blame the lady of the house, Granny, for all of this. She's an adult and should know better. Besides, does she really want a cat that's not going to protect her house from scurrying or flying creatures? Oscar voters noticed the plight that Sylvester was in and awarded three of his cartoons with Academy Awards, validating his spot as one of cartoons' all-time coolest cats.

1) Garfield

By far the cattiest of all cartoon cats and just the coolest of the cool. All he wants to do is eat and sleep and has nothing but utter disdain for his roommates. In all fairness though, he was saddled with two lousy ones. Odie is a dork and Arbuckle is even worse. Jon is lucky his pets can't fend for themselves, otherwise I'm sure they'd leave his sorry ass. Look, Garfield hates Mondays and downs lasagna like he lives in North Jersey, there's a reason why the cartoon is named after him and is top cat on my list.

Take a Catwalk with Me

Katie Haegele

Up the street from me and Joe is a small apartment building that used to be the Catholic school, which sits right behind the huge, gothic stone church. While I'll never set foot in a Catholic school again even if you paid me to, I admit that this place looks pretty cozy for the people who live there. When we pass by we can see their potted plants, strings of lights, glowing TV screens. And for a few months last year, if we remembered to look up to the third floor window, we'd see the "St. Clare's kitten," tiny and orange, looking down at us with his bright eyes.

St. Clare's used to have a big black cat on the first floor, too. The low windows of the bottom floor let you look straight down into the rooms, so the curtains are almost always drawn. For a few years a huge black cat slept on a windowsill in front of a closed curtain, so close you could touch him, his rounded back pressed against the window. I never once saw his face.

Also on our block is Pumpkin Spice, our nickname for her because of her brown, orange, and black calico coloring. She seems to be someone's pet, but she likes to be out on the prowl and can often be spotted hustling across the street or disappearing into one of the narrow alleyways between houses. She favors the block's quietest spots, including the low stone wall in our backyard, where she sleeps and suns herself for hours at a time.

The woman who organizes the farmer's market lives a few blocks over, in a lovely small house with a low front porch. She keeps a couch out there and a chalkboard that bears a new uplifting quote each week, plus a couple of very chill black cats. "Flat cat!" I shout whenever I spot one of the deflated felines draped over the couch.

Walking up the steep hill on that same block we might come upon Morris, a sweet grey tabby with black stripes. This is always fun. Morris is only ever seen being walked on a leash by his owner, a mellow, youngish man who must be very shy because he constantly watches movies on his phone and usually won't look up at us as we pass. Because of this we don't want to bother them, but we always coo over Morris (we'll say "hey buddy!" or "aww" in quiet voices as we pass) and we've recently been rewarded with a small glance and a smile from his human.

Seamus! This cat rules. He's a large, majestic looking creature with long fur that sweeps back from his face and chest like a beard. We've only ever seen him framed by the front window of the stately stone house he lives in, looking out and surveying the street solemnly like an old Irish fisherman gazing out at the sea. Seamus.

We often like to take Acorn, the street alongside the railroad trestle, because we can get a good view looking out over the bridge. If, on our stroll, we make it all the way to the far end of the block, we might luck out and see Acorn Boy. Acorn Boy is a dark colored cat who lives in the basement apartment of a two-story building that sits where the street dead-ends at a quiet wooded area. The building is shaded by the trees, and we don't know for sure what color Acorn Boy is because he sleeps on a windowsill that's always half dark. Somehow this mystery makes it feel like an even bigger treat to see his round shape through the glass, letting us know all is right with the world. Keep on keeping on, Acorn Boy.

NICE BOY.
PET-PET
OH SO CUTE.
PET-PET
SO SWEET.
PET-PET
SUCH SOFT FUR.
PET-PET
TURNING INTO A CAT...
OR A FURRY. ONE OR THE OTHER.
JDS '22

Meet the Contributors

Katie Haegele is a writer and the editor of this zine series. She misses her cat Coco every day, so it's a good thing there are lots of feline friends in the neighborhood for her to befriend. You can read more of her writing online at thelalatheory.com.

Alison Lee Chapman is an illustrator living and working in Philadelphia. She finds her inspiration in Wissahickon Valley Park, small neighborhood gardens, and watching her kids grow up. You can see more of her work at alisonleechapman.com or on Instagram @wolftreestudio.

Jo-Jo Sherrow is a visual artist, teacher, and musician residing in Philadelphia. Her zines include the *Captcha* series and *Healing Your Magical Body with Plants*.

Raymond E. Mingst is an artist, writer and curator (raymondemingst.com). He has exhibited, curated, and collaborated with numerous galleries and institutions. He co-founded Curious Matter, a contemporary art gallery located in Jersey City, NJ (curiousmatter.org). For occasional news and posts regarding his art practice and other diversions, Instagram is a place to find him. (@raymondemingst)

Andrew Keller is a recent convert to cat-lover status. He really had no idea how great cats were until one showed up in his backyard and wormed her way into his heart. Andrew writes music under the name Snow Caps (@snow__caps).

Ivan Dellinger is a writer, artist and performer living in Philadelphia. He has been drawing The Crime Cats daily since April 26th, 2022. You can find more crime cats on his instagram @capybaras and find his other work at linktr.ee/capybarazz

Ed Kemp lives in beautiful Downtown Jersey City in an apartment he shares with the coolest of cool cats, a chatty grey, white and black male tabby named Ashes. Rescued from the Jersey City incinerator, Ashes has been helping make zines for 10 years now, and co-running The Word Distro since starting up back in 2014. Some of their work includes the zines series *Pencil of the Week* and *Touring America*.

Keiko Ishibashi is an artist and musician from Athens, GA.

Joe Carlough (he/him) did the layout for this zine and designed the cover. He runs Displaced Snail Zines & Records. Find him on Instagram @displacedsnail or at displacedsnail.com

SUBSCRIBE!

For as little as $15/month, you can support a small, independent publisher and get every book that we publish—delivered to your doorstep!

www.Microcosm.Pub/BFF

Keep your cat parties going at www.Microcosm.Pub